Unesco and its programme

Youth and literacy:

you've got a ticket to ride

by Arthur Gillette

Unesco/UNCESI
Paris/New York 1972

1972 International
Book Year

Published by the United Nations
Educational, Scientific and Cultural Organization
Place de Fontenoy, 75700 Paris,
and the United Nations Centre
for Economic and Social Information,
New York, N. Y. 10017
Printed by L. P.-F. Léonard Danel, Loos

Printed in France   COM.71 /II.33 /A

Preface

This booklet appears as the result of co-operation between Unesco and the United Nations Centre for Economic and Social Information and between the Unesco Literacy Division and the Youth Division. Written for, as well as about, young people to underline the importance of youth's contribution to literacy work, it is intended to be thought-provoking. Not all the range of views, sometimes in conflict, which are outlined necessarily reflect the complete viewpoint of the author, of CESI or of Unesco.

Contents

We cannot afford to build two nations within the same territorial boundaries . . . one rich, educated . . . and the other, which constitutes the majority of the population, poor and illiterate.

From *The Common Man's Charter,* a declaration by students at Makerere University, Uganda, 1970.

You've got a ticket to ride[1]

What if you were illiterate?

Imagine, for a moment, that you woke up this morning illiterate. During the night you somehow mislaid the ability to read, write and count.

As an illiterate, how would you care for yourself, or get around, or send and receive information beyond the range of your voice and ears?

You would probably learn to survive in time, after a fashion. A few years ago, an illiterate Paris woman explained to a magazine writer that she had learned to navigate the Métro more or less successfully by memorizing the pictures portrayed on advertising posters at different stations. Each time the posters were changed, however, she had to start all over again; and she complained that, nowadays, posters are changed much more frequently than when she was young.

But even if you did adapt to your plight, illiteracy would remain a severe handicap in the modern world. To begin with, the trivia of everyday life would become infinitely problematic. And what about the more important things?

What kind of a job could you do? What kind of home—in terms of ideas as well as things—would your children grow up in? How would you record your thoughts, activities and plans? How would you communicate them to other people?

How would you find out what happened in the world yesterday, last week or 1,000 years ago? How would you find out what is likely to happen tomorrow, next year or a century from now?

1. With thanks (or apologies, as appropriate) to Messrs Lennon and McCartney.

The 'Gutenberg hang-up' or a 'weapon of liberation'?

To be sure, there is an increasing variety of means other than literacy for acquiring, storing and disseminating knowledge. It is true, too, that books are not always a very effective means of communication: a year from now you will probably have forgotten the very title of this booklet, for instance. It is fashionable to look on literacy as 'the Gutenberg hang-up'. Some specialists even predict that new electronic media will sooner than later replace 'outmoded' ways of exchange of information and ideas such as reading and writing.

Whether such a development is probable (or desirable) may be debated. What is certain, however, is that in the foreseeable future literacy will remain an indispensable vehicle for communication. It will also continue to offer literate individuals and groups an opportunity to shape the life they live rather than be subjugated to it. In this sense, literacy is a potential weapon of personal and social liberation.

If you were illiterate, you would lack one (though not the only) basic means for knowing and understanding the world, for benefiting from it and contributing to it. You would be a non-participant. Literacy is your 'ticket to ride' on Spaceship Earth as it hurtles toward the twenty-first century.

What, then, can be made of the hard fact that those with no ticket to ride number 783 million? This is the total—more than one-third of the world's adult population—of illiterates in 1972.

Why this booklet?

A glance at the crammed shelves and overflowing 'in' baskets of the Literacy Division at Unesco's Headquarters in Paris proves that there is a large and growing number of publications on world literacy. Why, then, add to the already unwieldy mass of printed words on this subject? Because, to date, there has been in this field no publication of international scope both for and about young people. *Youth and Literacy* . . . is meant to fill that gap.

What are the purposes, audience and organization of *Youth and Literacy* . . .?

The booklet has three purposes.

To be illiterate is to be a non-participant in today's world.

First, it presents and explains some of the basic facts of illiteracy and of literacy action. (A 'basic fact' presented above, for example, is that one-third of the world's adults are illiterate.) In what follows, the basic facts will focus on illiteracy and literacy as they affect youth—and as they are affected by youth.

Second, the booklet raises and analyses some of the major unresolved issues of illiteracy and literacy. Although the booklet takes a stand on some of them, diverse points of view are expressed. Where there is contradiction, the clashing points of view generally emerge from two opposing trends of attitudes and values visible among youth today.

Of these trends, one is the sceptical or 'cool' trend. Young people in this group are not necessarily cynical, but they do tend to smile at high-sounding pronouncements. They doubt that human beings can change very much. They feel that 'progress' is a pretty unrealistic idea. Their ideal—in so far as they have one—is 'live and let live'.

The other—and opposite—trend is that of protest. The young protesters are not necessarily fanatics. But they do display impatience and, at times, intransigence. They cannot sit idly by when faced with what they consider to be suffering and exploitation. And they demand change now.

These are admittedly extreme trends, in which only a minority of young people take part. But the expression of their respective points of view should help clarify—if not resolve—the issues raised below.

The third purpose of *Youth and Literacy* . . . is to stimulate and facilitate action by youth in favour of literacy. 'Action' of many kinds is called for. This means actual teaching of the three R's to illiterates. It also signifies support activities ranging from fund-raising to political action.

The audience for which the booklet has been written is, first and foremost, young people. This includes young workers and farmers as well as students; members of youth movements or organizations as well as those who aren't; inhabitants of developing nations as well as of industrialized countries; and conservatives and revolutionaries in addition to reformists and the apolitical.

This is a very diverse group. But its members have one thing in common, in addition to their age and the curiosity to pick up this booklet, they can read. They are privileged and therefore responsible for aiding the less privileged.

Youth leaders, teachers, journalists, parents and other adults concerned with the aspirations, activities and problems of young people form the other category of readers for whom the booklet is intended.

The booklet is organized in six chapters.

The first chapter defines and describes illiteracy and literacy, with special reference to the role of literacy in development.

Chapters II, III and IV show how young people are currently involved in literacy action as learners, teachers and supporters.

Chapter V briefly evaluates the results of youth's efforts in favour of literacy. It also ventures to make a few projections about possible lines for increased involvement of youth in literacy action in the future.

Chapter VI outlines concretely what you can do, directly and indirectly, to enhance literacy work in your country and elsewhere.

You've got your 'ticket to ride'; do you care about those who don't? If so, read on.

I   Youth and literacy

What is illiteracy?

Illiteracy is:

A middle-level worker in the State tomato juice cannery at Bagui-
neda, nineteen miles from Bamako (capital of the Republic of
Mali), in 1969. He was unable to sign for in-coming material,
make out accounts or check-lists, draw up invoices, receive or
give written instructions, keep track of the number and weight
of out-going crates, or grasp and remember technical explanations.

Nineteen million people over the age of 15 in Europe who can't
read or write.

'Far more difficult [to combat] than landing on the moon,' according
to the United States Assistant-Secretary for Education, J. E. Allen.

Over one-quarter of adults in Colombia, over three-quarters of
adults in Algeria, over one-half of adults in Turkey are illiterate.

A peasant and his wife at a bus-stop in Havana, Cuba, 1958, who
wait four hours because they can't read the destination signs
on the passing buses—and are too ashamed of their inability to
ask directions of passers-by, none of whom volunteer to help.

'Many millions of men who, because they are illiterate, are left
aside in the socio-economic development of the world and their
countries, the victims of an abiding discrimination which
condemns them to a life of ignorance.' (Pope Paul VI.)

A declining *percentage* of the world's population, but a growing
number of men and women.

Eradicable, in the opinion of René Maheu, Director-General of
Unesco, because 'The resources, both human and material, exist;
and where there is a will, there is a way.'

Perversely tenacious at literacy courses for foreign workers in
France. In the instructors' words:

WORLD ADULT POPULATION

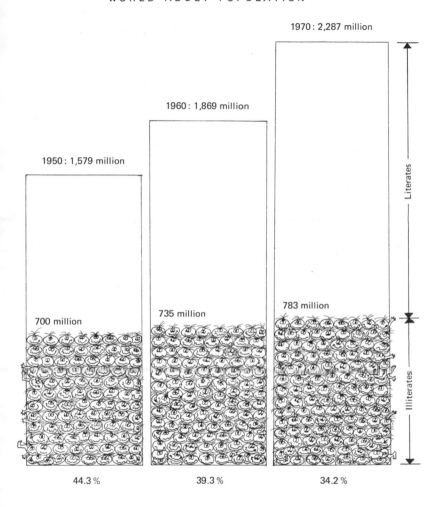

1970 : 2,287 million

1960 : 1,869 million

1950 : 1,579 million

700 million

735 million

783 million

Literates

Illiterates

44.3 %

39.3 %

34.2 %

A declining percentage of illiteracy, but a growing number of people.

'Pupils, after two or three months, are incapable of reading single words';

'A man, 30 to 40 years old, can't get the stuff into his head';

'A student who comes to every class: after a year and a half recognizes a grand total of 99 words';

'One group leader [older] gives up'.

Particularly widespread among women. Of adult men, 28 per cent are illiterate; the figure for women is 40.3 per cent.

Thirteen million more Indian illiterates in 1961 than in 1951, and 23 million more in 1970 than in 1961.

A woman in Addis Ababa, Ethiopia, in 1968: her baby is very ill. She rushes to the doctor, who gives her a phial of drops and tells her the proper dosage. Because she is upset, she forgets the dosage by the time she arrives home. The baby is nearly dead before she can find a neighbour to read the label on the phial.

The case against illiteracy

How can you make some order out of this kaleidoscope of facts and figures, opinions and vignettes? What patterns emerge? What are the main economic, social, political and cultural effects of illiteracy?

Assume illiteracy is on trial. With what crimes has the accused been charged? What points does the public prosecutor hammer home as he paces up and down between the bench and jury box, glowering occasionally in the direction of the prisoner's dock?

Being a man of the law, he begins with a legal argument: illiteracy is a flagrant denial of human rights.

The right of all to education was solemnly proclaimed by the Universal Charter of Human Rights in 1948. A number of countries have also seen fit to guarantee it by law or in their national constitutions. But this theoretical right is far from being a reality when more than one-third of the world's adult population is deprived of the most basic tools of education. And it is not likely to become a reality in the near future, since millions of today's infants will grow through childhood and adolescence into adulthood without receiving any kind of organized and modern education.

Illiteracy is more than a violation of the right to education. It also inhibits or prevents the effective exercise of other human rights, making a mockery of the Universal Declaration's affirmation that 'everyone is entitled to all the rights and freedoms' set forth in it. Illiteracy subverts the free choice of work, for example. If you couldn't read and write, the range of jobs open to you would be limited to the most degrading and exhausting forms of menial labour.

The Universal Declaration further proclaims that all 'are entitled without any discrimination to equal protection of the law'. Have you ever seen an illiterate person on trial? It is a sobering experience.

He can't read the law he is accused of having broken. He can't follow the documents concerned with his case. He can't verify that the transcript is being kept accurately. And if he lands in prison, he is totally dependent on others to appeal his conviction.

It is, in fact, quite likely that innocent illiterates have been convicted and imprisoned or executed who, had they been able to read and write, could have proven their innocence.

The second charge against illiteracy is that it favours exploitation. To make his case on this count, our public prosecutor might use the following evidence.

About two hours drive from Dakar (the capital) into the interior of the Republic of Senegal, and ten cross-country miles off the hardtop highway, stands a circle of huts shaded by venerable baobab trees. This is the hamlet of Keur Demba Anta (Uncle Anta's House). The 300 villagers who live there grow their own food. But to obtain cash to buy tools, clothes, household utensils and the like they must sell some of their produce outside. For this purpose, they cultivate ground-nuts, which they take in carts to a near-by market town. There they sell their crop to middlemen who resell it in Dakar.

Until recently, all the villagers were illiterate. And they had the distinct impression that Keur Demba Anta was not prospering as much as a near-by hamlet, which boasted a school.

Why, the farmers wondered, do our neighbours earn more with their ground-nuts than we do with ours? Our villages are the same size; the land is identical. We plant harvest in the same way. Surely we are not more stupid than they are! Yet their wives wear finer *boubous* than ours. They can afford sandals for their children. And they even bought an ox-cart last year, while we have to rent one to take our crops to market.

The answer was simple enough, as the people of Keur Demba Anta discovered when they began to learn to read, write and count.

17

The middleman was cheating them. Unlike their neighbours, they could not read the numbers on his scale, or do basic arithmetic, so he underpaid them per kilo of ground-nuts delivered. The third accusation levelled against illiteracy is that it favours undemocratic government.

If scribes have not always served the powerful, the powerful have almost always been served by scribes In many traditional societies (and some modern ones as well), the literate or lettered minority caste survives by dint of subservience to authorities who care nothing for the well-being of the majority. In such cases, pen and sword join forces to oppress. To spread literacy, and attempt to ensure its free use, become subversive acts.

In some liberal societies, literacy requirements have survived as a prerequisite for voting. The criteria for such requirements are determined by the literate, and the literate decide whether or not the criteria are met by those desiring to vote. This system makes possible the disenfranchisement of people for racial or other reasons.

Even where literacy requirements are fairly administered, their effect—and perhaps underlying intent—is to prevent those people who would benefit most by a change in the *status quo* from acting legally to change it.

Some countries are seeking to ensure more complete and more effective participation of citizens in making decisions that affect them at various levels. Here, illiteracy weakens the process of genuine democratization. It hampers the circulation and discussion of facts, ideas, plans and grievances. The illiterate citizen garners much of his information from hearsay. Even when he has heard a political leader on the radio or in person, he must rely on memory alone to provide food for thought a day or a year later.

He feels left out, confused, inferior, subjected to—rather than a participant in—the decisions made by the literates. When it comes to implementing these decisions that are not his, he is alienated or apathetic.

In sum, he is almost as surely disenfranchised as if there were a literacy requirement for the exercise of civic rights.

The public prosecutor might adopt a less rhetorical tone to plead the fourth charge against illiteracy—that it inhibits development. The most suitable materials for building this argument are the nuts and bolts of sociological and economic logic.

Development is motion. It is societies changing and economies growing.

For societies to change, old truths must be questioned and outmoded institutions must be dismantled. For old truths to be questioned, there must be ready access to new ideas. For outmoded institutions to be dismantled, alternatives must be invented and constructed. Illiteracy restricts access to new ideas and slows the invention and construction of alternative institutions.

For economies to grow, old (slow, inefficient and expensive) techniques must be replaced with new (quick, rational and cheap) techniques. To replace the old techniques there must be circulation of the new. For circulation of new techniques to be successful, recipients must be able to understand them and use them independently. Illiteracy prevents the successful circulation of new techniques.

For example, you want to build a house. To determine the appropriate size, shape, style and cost of the house, you consult a wide range of books and magazines and perhaps write to an architect. Among the various solutions your digging has unearthed you choose a rather nice prefabricated model. Local builders are not familiar with prefabrication methods, but they read up on them and, when construction gets under way, follow the blueprints carefully.

Without literacy the house would have taken much longer to build—and might have proved impossible.

Picture development as a boat, illiteracy as an anchor. A boat cannot sail while its anchor is down.

The fifth count against illiteracy is that it hampers culture.

In the first place, the storage of much of the world's cultural heritage would have been impossible without reading and writing. Homer, for instance, was illiterate. If someone hadn't transcribed the stories he told, images like 'the wine-dark sea' and 'rosy-fingered dawn' would have been lost to us for ever. In the second place, cinema, radio, television and other devices notwithstanding, the written word remains the chief medium of diffusing culture to broad audiences. It is still the main link joining creators and consumers of literature, criticism and many other cultural forms; and an important tool enabling consumers of culture to become creators in their own right.

At this point, our public prosecutor would pause and clear his throat to heighten the effect of his final argument, which summarizes all the others—that illiteracy undermines social peace.

What are the causes of war? The denial of human rights leads to uprisings; exploitation results in revolt; undemocratic governments must be overthrown; underdevelopment engenders the increasingly violent struggle for development; and exclusion from culture calls forth the non-negotiable demand for admission to written culture.

Internationally, too, illiteracy undermines peace. It prevents circulation of factual information between different races, nations and civilizations. It limits mutual knowledge and understanding, while heightening mutual suspicion and aggression.

In all these ways, illiteracy acts as a war-monger.

A sceptic's retort

The prosecution rests its case here. But to give illiteracy a fair trial and get as close as possible to the truth, sceptical comments on the arguments just advanced must be made. After them the prosecution will be given the floor anew for rebuttal.

First, a sceptic would most certainly question the assumptions on which the case against illiteracy seems to rest. With reference to the first argument, for instance, he would point out that while there are violations of human rights in countries with high illiteracy rates, the same rights are also denied in countries with universal literacy.

The same can be said of literacy and exploitation. People who can read may be much more readily subjected to commercial and political propaganda and cowed into accepting an exploitative social and economic hierarchy. As for defending oneself against undemocratic government, the case for literacy seems even weaker. Fascism flourishes in societies with high literacy rates. It reached its greatest degree of diabolical perfection in Germany, a country with universal literacy and a long record of respect for and creation of the written word.

A sceptic might well concede that literacy and development go hand in hand. But he would ask: Development for what?

To ensure the storage and dissemination of culture? Ah, but that implies that predominantly literate societies are somehow 'better' than predominantly illiterate ones—which leads into the old trap of ethnocentrism. Surely, societies that drop atomic weapons on each other are not more civilized or less primitive than societies without nuclear capability simply because they can read and write.

Perhaps development for peace, then? 'Peace and progress' are often linked in the speeches and writings of world leaders. But some studies suggest an inverse correlation between progress and peace; that is, the more you have progress the less likely you are to have peace. A man who has little, and no hope of getting more, will make do with his modest lot and live a fairly contented life, leaving his equally impoverished neighbours in peace. But tantalize him with the view of wealthy neighbours and he will not long remain passive. And the more he 'develops' the more he will refine his weapons. This is the century of mass literacy—it is also the century when, thanks in part to mass literacy, man has created the means of blowing himself and his world into cosmic dust.

How would the public prosecutor reply to the sceptic's arguments? He might begin by making a fine—but important—distinction. His job was to make a case against illiteracy, not to make one for literacy.

He said that illiteracy denies human rights, for example, but did not affirm that literacy guarantees human rights. He pointed out that illiteracy facilitates exploitation and undemocratic government, but did not suggest that literacy necessarily makes for a democratic society free of exploitation. And so on.

We are dealing with possibilities and potentialities rather than measurable causes and effects. The goal is to open new channels for the realization of man's potential. How those channels are used is, naturally, another question. For many organizers, teachers and learners, literacy work is admittedly an act of faith. Of faith that, like all education, literacy will ultimately be used for constructive rather than destructive purposes.

Would it be wiser to sit by and do nothing?

The answer may not be immediately apparent to all—certainly not to the sceptics! Perhaps the time has come, now that we have tried to answer the question 'What is illiteracy?', to approach the problem from another angle by asking 'What is literacy'?

Literacy : past, present and future

What, exactly, is literacy? From shotgunning to sharpshooting

A few months ago, a middle-aged man entered the labour exchange of a Central American city in search of work.

'Can you read and write?' was the first question of the young woman behind the desk.

Standing very straight, the man proudly replied, 'I am literate, *señorita!*'.

'But can you read and write?' the girl insisted.

Was she hard of hearing? Not at all; they were in fact talking about two different things. Until recently, a widespread definition of literacy in this particular .area was the ability to scrawl one's name . . . and that's all. Signing his name gave the man considerable prestige in his home village, where most people were totally illiterate. But it was hardly sufficient to enable him to do a job requiring reading and writing.

Another extreme is suggested by the confusion sometimes made in French between *analphabète* and *illettré*. The first means 'illiterate' in the sense of 'unable to read or write', while the second can also imply a lack of erudition. Where, between the extremes of tracing a shaky signature and creating *War and Peace*, does a reasonable and useful definition of literacy lie'.

In 1951 a Unesco committee devised a solution by suggesting that a person is literate when he can 'both read, with understanding, and write a short simple statement on his daily life'.

To this has often been added, in practice, a basic familiarity with addition, subtraction, multiplication and division. In Keur Demba Anta, the Senegalese village described above, literacy work stressed arithmetic linked to the use of an abacus as the most necessary skill for keeping track of their ground-nut crops.

Literacy work with adults has not always been so closely geared to local conditions. Although it has existed for some time, it only began to gain prominence after the First World War, using what is known as the mass approach. The mass approach sought to teach the greatest possible number of illiterates, often treating them as isolated entities separated from their environment. It tended to use teachers and books straight from the primary school. And it was looked on, by economists and governments, as a consumption or luxury item in national budgets; that is, it was thought that money spent on literacy was like water poured down the drain—lost for ever.

In the late 1950s and early 1960s, many Afro-Asian countries won independence. Masters at last in their own homes, they began to make an inventory of the education systems left by retreating colonial powers. They soon realized that education could play a much greater role than previously in narrowing the widening gap between rich countries and poor.

The mass approach to literacy, for example, was found deficient in several ways. By 'shotgunning' reading and writing, it dispersed and often wasted its efforts. By considering pupils in isolation from their environment, it did not teach them skills of immediate and practical use. By mobilizing school-teachers and materials, it tended to treat adults as children. And by viewing literacy as a consumption item, it limited the funds available from national budgets, which could ill afford to waste money on luxuries.

Ins um, it was no longer felt possible to pour water down the drain.

At the national and international levels, a new approach to literacy began to emerge from this analysis of the mass strategy. Baptized the 'selective, functional and work-oriented approach', the new strategy is not a miracle solution. Nor does it claim to be the only valid way to organize literacy work. But it does mark something of a breakthrough.

Instead of 'shotgunning', the new strategy 'sharpshoots'. It concentrates on selected agricultural and industrial projects. Through adaptation of teaching methods and materials, farmers and workers are given literacy that is geared to actual on-the-job needs. It helps them solve real problems and widen actual bottlenecks. The goal is economic betterment both for the enterprise and for the learner. From a luxury or consumption article, literacy becomes a necessity, an item for priority investment.

In other words, the water that was once lost for ever down the drain is channelled so as to drive development.

This change in concept is reflected in a new definition of literacy—more complete than the 1951 effort quoted above—devised by another Unesco committee in 1962.

A person is literate when he has acquired the essential knowledge and skills which enable him to engage in all those activities in which literacy is required for effective functioning in his group or community, and whose attainments in reading, writing and arithmetic make it possible for him to continue to use these skills towards his own and the community's development.

Unesco had encouraged and aided literacy efforts since its creation in 1946. Now, it undertook to accelerate and focus action through an Experimental World Literacy Programme. Under this programme, the selective, functional and work-oriented literacy approach has been put into practice in twelve developing countries. In Iran, for instance, work has concentrated on the irrigated agricultural zone of Dezful and in the industrial region of Isfahan. In Tanzania (to mention but one other example) the programme combines literacy instruction with the promotion of co-operatives in the cotton-rich Mwanza region.[1]

How can this programme be evaluated? A young person of the protesting persuasion would doubtless be impatient with what has been achieved—or, rather, with what hasn't been achieved—to date.

He would point out that after years of meetings and missions, studies and reports—and despite an expenditure of many millions of dollars by national authorities and international agencies—the Experimental Programme has yet to produce more than a few thousand new literates. At the end of 1970, in fact, less than 180,000 adults were enrolled in literacy classes organized in the framework of the Experimental World Literacy Programme. In contrast there are about 10 million new adult illiterates each year in the world. In sum, the protester would say that a sharpshooter can't kill a herd of elephants.

A Unesco official might parry the protester's criticism in two ways. First, he would stress that the Unesco programme is just what its title says: experimental. It was never intended to be a world campaign for the total eradication of illiteracy—although it might some day lead to such a campaign. Secondly, he would say that the preparation of the various country projects had to be done with extreme care and took, therefore, rather longer than expected. Literacy had to be adapted to the needs and possibilities of different administrative and co-ordinating structures. Educational materials

---

1. The other countries participating in the Experimental World Literacy Programme are: Algeria, Ecuador, Ethiopia, Guinea, India, Madagascar, Mali, Sudan, the Syrian Arab Republic and Venezuela.

suitable for adults had to be devised and tested. Also, a number of unforeseen changes in the political and/or economic situation have taken place in some countries.

In rebuttal, the protester might simply shrug his shoulders and recall the words of Unesco's Director-General: 'The resources, both human and material, exist; where there is a will, there is a way.'

Part of the problem, of course, is lack of money. Despite Unesco's efforts in this field, the increase in funds allotted to literacy efforts has been far from spectacular.

There have been some advances, to be sure. Between 1967 and 1969, for instance, only four countries replying to a Unesco survey had reduced spending and eleven reported no change, while sixteen had increased their efforts. Nevertheless, funds for literacy have generally remained an infinitesimal part of national budgets, often less than one-tenth of 1 per cent.

Compare this to expenditure on armaments and high outlays for other sectors, considered by many to be non-essential. At the rate of U.S.$10 to make a person literate (an approximate but reasonable figure), adult illiteracy in the world could be easily wiped out with the price of a single three-man moon shot.

In addition to faring miserably in national budgets, literacy is only a very poor cousin to schooling in education budgets. It tends to hover between 0.5 and 1.5 per cent of education spending.

The same trend seems to apply to literacy's share of international assistance to developing countries. According to the Organization for Economic Co-operation and Development (OECD), aid to education 'accounts for about 10 per cent of the total official [government-to-government] bilateral flow of resources to developing countries' from the sixteen nations belonging to its Development Assistance Committee. Figures on the percentage of educational aid allocated to literacy are difficult to come by, but it clearly does not stand among the priority areas of assistance.

Governments and private sources would doubtless accord a higher priority if they were convinced that literacy contributes measurably and decisively to development. Does it?

If underdevelopment is a vicious circle, is literacy the chicken or the egg?

Literacy and development:
cart and horse or chicken and egg?

A correlation between illiteracy and underdevelopment can be demonstrated. Poor countries are also illiterate countries while rich countries are literate. But what is the exact nature of the relationship between literacy and development?

It was stated above that literacy has come to be viewed as a necessary investment rather than an optional luxury. This implies that literacy (and education in general) is a horse pulling the cart of development. The actual relationship between literacy and development is probably better expressed as a chicken-and-egg dilemma.

The question may be asked thus: does literacy ignite development or does development make literacy possible? It seems that this is a mutual process. There is reciprocal acceleration or braking, depending on the kind and amount of literacy and development.

Literate workers are more productive than illiterates. Their work has a higher yield per man-hour. Thus, through a process known as capital accumulation, more money becomes available for reinvestment in things like literacy. Which, in turn, enables other workers to become literate and more productive, triggering the process anew. So, it seems to take a literate society to make a literate society.

In practice, this riddle may be less bothersome than it looks on paper. After all, the Industrial Revolution happened in Europe and North America in step with the gradual spread of primary education. Indeed, given the experience of the nineteenth century, a sceptic might question the urgency of adult literacy. Why not continue the present priority on primary schooling until illiteracy dies out?

The answer is clear: there is no time.

Thanks to the technology produced by the Industrial Revolution, particularly medical technology, the world's population has grown more in the last 150 years than in the previous 10,000. It will probably double again in the next thirty-five years. But world production of food, goods and services is barely, if at all, keeping pace with this 'galloping demography'. In some places, production has already fallen behind. There are countries in Latin America, for instance, where the calory intake *per capita* is lower in 1971 than it was in 1800.

To expect schooling alone to win the race against time would be for the hare of development to doze by the wayside while the tortoise of starvation slowly but surely catches up.

It might be a different story if formal education were more suited to the needs of the Third World. But it isn't. Despite a decade or more of adaptive efforts, schooling in Asia, Africa and Latin America still tends often to be: very expensive; unable to meet the demand for mass education; unlinked to local realities and needs; pedagogically off-putting and ineffective in transmitting information, ideas and skills; and incomplete in that adulthood begins where school stops, whereas there is an urgent need periodically to refresh old knowledge and provide new.

Literacy does not have all the answers. But, especially as practised under the selective, functional and work-oriented approach, it is geared toward meeting the demand for education among the unschooled masses; offers more direct economic returns sooner; adapts its contents to local needs; uses more attractive and effective pedagogy; and, while providing basic adult education, also lays the foundation for continuing education. For many, literacy can be the launch-pad for lifelong education.

And it may just turn out that lifelong education will enable the hare of development, rather than the tortoise of starvation, to cross the finishing line first.

II   Youth learning

Part of the problem or part of the solution?

You are probably wondering what all of this has to do with youth. So far we've been talking about adult illiteracy and adult education, about schools (which tend to be adult-run) and governments (ditto—only more so).

A protester would affirm that illiteracy is injustice, and that young people care about injustice. In answer, a sceptic might purse his lips doubtfully. . . . To which a protester would reply that some young people care about injustice, and that the rest ought to.

Be that as it may, illiteracy and literacy do concern young people, in two ways. First, young people are part of the problem when they are illiterate themselves. Second, they are part of the solution when they play any one of three roles in literacy programmes: when they take the time and make the effort to learn how to read and write, if they are illiterate; when, if they are literate, they teach literacy; and when, also literate, they organize supporting activities for literacy programmes.

The next three chapters of *Youth and Literacy* . . . focus, in turn, on young people in literacy action as learners (this chapter), teachers (Chapter III), and supporters (Chapter IV).

The phrase 'adult illiteracy' used so frequently above is admittedly imprecise. It applies to illiterates in the economically active sector of the population, that is to say, people above the age of 15.

Assume that 'youth' includes the 15–24 age group. A few figures suffice to bring home the extent of illiteracy at this age level. In Colombia 18.5 per cent of the 15–24 cohort cannot read or write. In Algeria the figure is 55 per cent, while in Libya it reaches 62.3 per

Drop-outs from the educational race: an enormous wastage.

cent. In the view of the United Nations Economic Commission for Africa, part of 'the main general problem facing the countries in Africa is that great numbers of young people have reached adolescence without any schooling, or with only a short period of primary education . . . ' and are, therefore, illiterate.

To express these generalities in human terms, we shall now focus on representative youthful illiterates; some major issues facing people in various groups of illiterates will be raised; and some examples of literacy programmes designed for them will be described.

School drop-outs : 'social dynamite'

A report on early school-leavers by the world office of the Young Women's Christian Association calls school drop-outs 'social dynamite'. Why? First, because the problem is much more acute than generally imagined, as the following comparison shows.

Among every 100 Europeans born in 1945, 96 entered primary school (four died before the age of 5), 93 completed primary school and 81 went on to the first stage of secondary education. In sub-Saharan Africa, on the other hand, only 38 of the 79 children who survived to the age of 5 out of each 100 born in 1945 entered primary school. Only 16 completed four years, 12 finished primary school and 5 went on to a secondary education.

Calculating conservatively, these figures mean that only about one in three Africans who enter primary school (already a minority) stay there long enough to retain what they have learned. The drop-out rates in the rest of the Third World are, on the whole, not radically different; and those who drop out of school tend also to drop out of society.

If all the wasted energies, dashed hopes and bitter frustrations generated by this process could be captured and bottled, they would make an explosive force of incredible magnitude—'social dynamite' indeed!

The situation would be less dramatic if, during the short time they spend at school, drop-outs learned skills that they could put to immediate use when they leave the classroom. Such practical schooling is rare, however. In most cases formal education continues to produce round pegs, while society is made up of square holes.

31

The chief function of many Third World primary schools is to prepare pupils to enter secondary education, which in turn is designed to facilitate matriculation to university. When out of 1,000 pupils entering primary school only one reaches university, the system can only be termed élitist. When unemployment among university graduates—technical and scientific as well as liberal arts—continues to grow, this élitism can only be called absurd.

Even where education has been reformed so as to produce leavers with practical skills at lower levels, its relation to the actual job market is seldom close. The tendency is to turn out an abundance of middle-level, white-collar workers, while the number of jobs for such people remains stationary or declines.

A sceptic might conclude from this analysis that it would be wiser to reduce rather than increase literacy action until the labour market can absorb more literates. From an economist's point of view, on the other hand, school drop-outs who relapse into illiteracy are wasting the previous investment in their education. Somehow, this enormous waste must be prevented.

Recycling human resources

Rich countries are increasingly attempting to reduce wastage of natural resources by re-using tin cans, newspapers and the like. In the same way more and more poor countries are attempting to recycle their human resources through special programmes designed partly or wholly for young school drop-outs. One such programme is the Kenya National Youth Service.

Any national holiday in Kenya sees a contingent of young men and women from all parts of the country marching smartly through the flower-bedecked main avenues of Nairobi. From afar, you might mistake them for soldiers. Look more closely and you will see that the sun is glinting off shovel blades, not rifle barrels. The group belongs to the Kenya National Youth Service (KNYS).

At any given time, KNYS mobilizes 3,000–4,000 young volunteers, many of them illiterate and semi-literate school drop-outs. During their eighteen-month tour of duty, servicemen and women do two things. First, they resume their education. They can choose among maths, science, civics, history and a variety of trades, from electricity to auto-mechanics. Second, they take part in work projects including bush clearing, dam building, irrigation and house construction. Some of the jobs completed to date have been worth several hundred thousand dollars.

Similar programmes exist in more than thirty developing countries. All face numerous problems: they can only accept a tiny number of the many young people eager to volunteer; they cannot guarantee employment on mustering out; they are sometimes expensive to run; and they are occasionally looked on as operations for taming justifiably rebellious youth. Despite their defects, civic-service programmes in many countries hold out just about the only hope for 'recycling' human resources that have been wasted by having to leave school prematurely.

Non-school-attenders

Sbr mftah el-janna—'patience is the key to paradise': this is one of the first sayings that many Algerian rural women teach their daughters. Nefissa, a 14-year-old from a mountain town 200 miles south of the Mediterranean coast, learned it years ago. It has proved an apt description of her life so far. At least, the 'patience' part has; 'paradise' is far removed from Nefissa's daily existence.

As soon as she could walk, she began to work. First came responsibility for feeding and dressing her younger brothers and sisters. Then spinning, washing and mending. Then caring for domestic animals, collecting clay and making household utensils. Then finding, cutting and carrying firewood. In smaller doses, these tasks might seem like play. But they are never-ending.

In such circumstances, patience may not lead to paradise, but resignation does make survival possible. The more so since, as a girl, Nefissa has always been compared unfavourably to her brothers and other male relatives. As a symbol of this subjugation to men, Nefissa—like many other girls of 14 in the Algerian countryside— began wearing a veil a few months ago.

Another indicator of her inferior status is her father's refusal to allow her to attend school. Despite Algerian Government policy, school attendance rates are much higher among boys than among girls. As a result, less than one-half of males between the ages of 15 and 19 are illiterate, while the figure for females in the same group is over 76 per cent.

If Nefissa ever has daughters, one of the first lessons she will teach them will be 'patience is the key to paradise'.

To reverse this trend . . .

Discrimination on the basis of sex is not the only reason why many young people never attend school. Lack of facilities is a major cause, particularly in the countryside. In many nations, urban youth has fairly ready access to education while rural young people are almost totally deprived.

Even where schools exist, their cost is often prohibitive. Free education is spreading, but many schools in developing countries still require tuition and /or other fees. Seemingly minor expenses can also be a stumbling block. Uniforms and school materials cost only a few shillings a year in East Africa, but this is an unbearable burden when the average *per capita* income is under U.S.$100—and where families tend to be large. Often, too, mere survival demands that families keep their children out of school to work.

All these and other reasons add up to a growing total of unschooled adult illiterates in the world. Each year the number of young people reaching 15 without having learned to read and write in primary school is greater than the number of people over 15 who have become literate. 'To reverse this trend', in the words of Unesco's Director-General, René Meheu, it would have been 'necessary between 1960 and 1970 to double the efforts made for the promotion of literacy during the previous decade.' The efforts were not doubled, and the trend was not reversed.

When 'A B C' spells 'Well'

In Upper Volta the trend will be particularly hard to reverse. Although 25 per cent of the national budget is allocated to education, schools can accommodate only 11 per cent of would-be pupils. Most of the school-attenders are boys. The girls grind millet, collect firewood and make daily trips on foot of as much as six miles to the nearest well to carry water in heavy earthen pitchers. So polluted is the water that dysentery, bilharzia and other energy-sapping illnesses are widespread.

To change this situation, the Upper Volta Government has begun a functional literacy programme focused on the concerns and needs of young rural women. In 1969 literacy classes were opened in fifteen villages of the region of Kongoussi, in the north of Upper Volta mid-way between Niger and Mali. Three mornings a week, classes meet to learn reading and writing in the *Mooré* language and other subjects.

If you happened through the village of, say, Luluka on a morning when such a class was taking place, you would see twenty women and girls seated in the shade of a thatched shelter. Before them stands a volunteer literacy instructor pointing out odd letters and a few phrases on a blackboard.

Although the pupils are beginners, you don't find among the phrases anything remotely resembling 'run, run and see'. This is functional literacy—tied to their everyday life. 'Dirty water kills babies', reads one pupil. Another pieces together, 'we could make 'a charcoal filter'. And a third: 'why do we walk so far to find water?

Here, literacy is not an end in itself. Rather, it is designed to lead to an awareness of problems and, from there, to practical solutions. A recent visitor to the Kongoussi region was told that 'A B C' spells "well" '. In ten of the fifteen pilot villages, the people have been stimulated by literacy classes to dig their own pure-water wells.

Clearly, this is just a beginning. There are several thousand villages in Upper Volta with similar needs. Yet—with one-quarter of its budget going to education—the government would be hard put to spend a great deal more on literacy. And, at present rates, foreign aid is not likely to bridge the gap between needs and resources. In Upper Volta as elsewhere, whether or not the trend toward increasing numbers of illiterates can be reversed is, at best, a moot question.

Young workers

Ayalyew K. considers himself lucky. He has a job. Almost alone among his circle of friends in their early twenties—and part of a tiny minority of the 25 million inhabitants of little-industrialized Ethiopia—he can count on regular pay as a mechanic in one of Addis Ababa's big garages. Beginning as an apprentice four years ago, at 18, he quickly caught on to the whims and peculiarities of

Lucky to have a job—but baffled by the instructions.

Land Rovers, Volkswagens, Moskviches and other makes prevalent in Ethiopia.

But, if he considers himself lucky, Ayalyew is also worried. He expects that some day, sooner or later, someone will come to the garage looking for a job who is not only a good mechanic—but who also knows how to read and write.

Being illiterate, Ayalyew uses pressure pumps, dip-sticks, feeler gauges and other tools and equipment with possibly dangerous inaccuracy. Also, when stumped by a problem, he can't refer directly to the well-thumbed owners' manuals lining one wall of the garage office. Each time, Ayaleyw has to ask the chief mechanic to read out the necessary information.

A sixty-shilling thumb-print

There are many theories about the place of employment in development. In general, today, the goal of 'capital intensive' operations predominates. Under it, modern equipment is sought (automated factories, mines and plantations) according to the principle that the higher profit margins thus accruing will make more money available for reinvestment. This is what might be called the 'tractor theory' of development. It requires fairly highly skilled workers (the tractor driver compared to the peasant using antiquated methods), but also less workers since each machine does the jobs of many men.

An alternative proposal is the 'labour-intensive' approach. Under it, stress would be increasingly laid on spreading employment—even if less sophisticated technology were used in the process. This could be called the 'improved-plough theory' of development. It stands a good chance to gain ground in the years to come, since population will probably continue to outrun available jobs.

According to figures of the International Labour Organisation (ILO), the working-age population of the developing countries is expected to increase by between 20 per cent and 32 per cent from 1970 to 1980. The number of new jobs available in manufacturing (to take but one sector) will probably only be able to absorb between 5 per cent and 10 per cent of the new entrants into the Third World labour force—if the present stress on capital-intensive methods continues.

Whether tractor-oriented or based on the improved plough,

employment will increasingly require workers with a modicum of education. In Algeria, great hopes are being put in the power of new steel, petrochemical and other industries to raise the national living standards. But the illiteracy of one-half of the country's labour force is looked on by the National Literacy Centre as a serious brake on such progress.

According to the centre, the effects of literacy are felt in the following five ways: (a) productivity is higher among literate workers; (b) they need less supervision; (c) they are more careful with machines and equipment; (d) they are less accident-prone; (c) they are more punctual.

From the point of view of the individual worker, there is another advantage in learning how to read and write—pay is generally higher. A few years ago, in the part of Tanzania then called Tanganyika, a literate worker was paid ninety shillings for a given job, while a man who could only sign with his thumb-print received thirty shillings for the same job. Because he could not read, the second man was cheated of sixty shillings.

Too few jobs—even for literates

Typical of the conditions and problems of much of the literacy work being carried on among workers is the crash campaign organized by the semi-governmental City Social Education Committee of Bombay.

At 4.30 p.m. any week-day, the city's many textile mills disgorge thousands of white-clad hands into the congested Central Zone. It becomes all but impossible to pass with any kind of vehicle—including a bicycle. Many of the workers head home. Still more linger in the streets to chat or stare at the latest cinema posters. Others—a growing number—gather hurriedly in their *chawls,* multi-storey tenement compounds that house up to 600 people each in rooms of up to 40 people (with an average of one water tap for every twenty rooms), for daily literacy classes.

Studying in an overcrowded room after a hard day's work is difficult. But it is precisely in the hope of being able to earn more and afford better housing that many *chawl*-dwellers have found the will to study. All too often, however, the hope of promotion is disappointed; then, the will to learn wanes. Only about one in ten literacy pupils continues into the all-important second-year course.

Why? A visit to one of the classes yields a possible answer—an answer that is hardly limited to India.

Twenty-five mill hands sit cross-legged on mats in a dingy room. Their faces are lit by a single bare bulb, dangling from the ceiling. Several of the faces look discouraged.

The teacher, an attractive graduate in her early twenties, translates your questions and her pupils' answers.

Why do they continue studying?

'I want to read more about other countries,' ventures one. There is silence while the others suck their pencils and think.

'I don't know,' one blurts out. 'I've learned to read and write letters, but that hasn't got me a better job.'

Why not?

'There are too few jobs—even for literates!'

Young farmers: 'dazzled, then disappointed'

It is asking a lot to hope that rural youth will want to stay in the countryside when facilities of health, education and amusement (if not employment) are better developed in urban areas; when the town is 'where the action is'. On the other hand, for a long time to come in many countries, development can't and won't equal urbanization. In these countries, development will probably grow from the improvement of old agriculture rather than from the creation of new industries. And illiteracy continues to be a stumbling block in the path of agricultural improvement.

It is not the only obstacle, however. Still more important are the worsening terms under which poor agricultural countries sell their produce to rich industrial ones. Ghana's case is typical. According to research carried out by the Haslemere Group (which is made up of Britons—many of them young—concerned with development), 'Two-thirds of Ghana's exports are cocoa. Between 1953 and 1961 cocoa exports [from Ghana] increased by 71 per cent in volume, but revenue only increased by 23 per cent because of declining prices on the world cocoa market. In sum, more goods for less money.

Spreading literacy among young farmers will not improve the terms of trade for agricultural articles, a sceptic would hasten to point out. A protester would retort that an improvement in the terms

The big city lights lure the migrant.

of trade would mean a better market for agricultural articles, which would stimulate greater production, which would require improved agriculture, which—in turn—would make the spread of literacy among rural youth indispensable.

Only then, it can be argued, would the countryside come alive, and become both attractive and profitable, thus slowing the rural exodus of people toward the towns. Until this happens, urban life will continue to spark that vague longing among Third World farm youth. And, in the words of a member of the Latin American secretariat of the International Movement of Catholic Agricultural and Rural Youth, young people fleeing the countryside will continue to be 'dazzled, then disappointed' by what they find in the towns.

Chickenfeed in the showers: a wise move

Realizing that world trade will not be reoriented overnight, some countries are experimenting with interim solutions. Mali, for example, is attempting to spur its agriculture by increasing and diversifying domestic consumption. To meet the need for better farmers, the government has created a number of rural activation centres.

This programme has grown out of an earlier, less flexible effort which seems to have hastened rather than slowed the flight of youngsters to towns. Under the new orientation, village boys come to rural activation centres to learn a variety of skills—including literacy—that are taught in such a way as to be of immediate and practical use. The goal is to encourage young farmers to stay in their villages—to become agents of improvement, both in agriculture and in community life.

The change from the old to the new approach has been thorough, you will discover if you visit one of the centres.

Scattered in the dazzling sun around a dusty assembly field are several low buildings. The centre's director takes you into one, a dormitory. Once your eyes are accustomed to the dark inside, you note with surprise that metal bedsteads are stacked in the corner, while at each boy's place there is only a rolled sleeping mat.

The director leads you outside again, and you encounter surprise number two. Hovering like a mantis over the centre's well is a petrol-powered water pump—but it is badly rusted and visibly has been out of action for months. Water is drawn, instead, by a crude crank-and-drum mechanism.

The biggest surprise comes at a building over whose door the words 'Sanitary block' have been partly crossed out. Inside, the showers are crammed with sacks of chicken-feed.

Outside again, you sit down in the shade of a mango bush with the director, who asks your impressions.

You tell him that you think there is considerable waste in the camp: the unused bedsteads, the showers, the rusting pump. . . .

'Yes,' he agrees, 'there is waste. But not because we don't use these things. The waste was in buying them in the first place.'

But why? Don't they represent steps toward a healthier, less toilsome life?

'Of course. But they are steps that lead straight to the towns. Our villages will only be able to afford such improvements a decade or more from now. So, if you teach a farm boy to sleep in a bed and use a shower, you. are pretty much guaranteeing that he will leave the village. It is better to teach him small improvements that he can make at home—like the crank-and-drum device for drawing water from the well. Deciding to use those showers to store chicken-feed was one of the wisest moves we've made.'

Young migrants

When he arrived in Switzerland from his native Tunisia eighteen months ago, Slimane wasn't sure what to expect. He had been hired sight unseen to work as a dishwasher in a Basle restaurant, and hoped that the pay would be enough to allow him to send money home each month. On the other hand, he wondered how he would manage in a country whose people and climate were so different from home.

In some ways he hasn't been disappointed. The pay is excellent—compared to Tunisia at least. But, on the whole, he has found adjustment difficult. One problem is that people in Basle assume that everyone can read. This assumption has handicapped Slimane —who is illiterate—and caused him embarrassment more than once.

Take the time he signed up at a driving school, for instance. Having heard that drivers were better paid than dishwashers, he decided. to get a driving licence. Everything went well as long as he was learning how to shift gears, park in tight spaces, and so on. Then came the awful day when his instructor handed him a little book and said: 'You're nearly ready for the licence test. All you've got to do is learn the simple rules of the road contained in this manual.'

Assimilation or adaptation?

Illiteracy is not only a problem of the Third World. Industrialized countries have illiterates too, right in their own backyards.

In Europe, today, there are some 27 million illiterates over the age of 15. Some, of course, are natives of the countries in which they live. Illiteracy has proved tenacious in southern Italy, for example, despite an energetic campaign. In Hungary, illiteracy among the semi-nomadic gypsy population has only recently been reduced to negligible proportions. And, in all countries, an as yet unmeasured percentage of school-leavers relapses into illiteracy for want of cultural stimulation.

It remains, however, that in most industrialized countries illiteracy is chiefly found among migrant workers.

The extent reached by international migration in recent years is not always realized. In the Federal Republic of Germany, there are 2 million foreign workers. In Switzerland, fully 18 per cent of the total population—and one-quarter of the labour force—is made up of migrant workers and their families. Nearly all workers migrating to France come from areas with high illiteracy rates: North Africa, sub-Saharan Africa, Portugal, Spain. A report issued by the French National Commission for Unesco estimates that roughly one-half of the 2 million economically active migrants are illiterate.

These are staggering figures—but the solution to the problem cannot come through quantitative action alone. It is not merely an issue of how many migrant workers should be given the chance to become literate. Why and how they should learn to read and write must also be taken into account.

The basic question is: assimilation or temporary adaptation? Should a young foreign worker settle and become a citizen of the country to which he has migrated, or should he ultimately return home?

It would be inhumane to force (or strongly encourage) migrants who have fled oppression to return to their native countries. On the other hand, many migrants leave home for economic rather than political reasons. And often their native countries are poor precisely because they lack manpower with the skills migrants learn in the country where they go to work. Is it fair, then, for rich countries to cream off the best-trained workers from poor countries?

Exactly how can literacy courses best enable migrants to adapt temporarily to the new country, while preparing to return to the old? For example, should Slimane learn to read and write in German (the language of Basle), or French (widespread in both Switzerland and Tunisia), or Arabic (his mother tongue), or two of these, or all three?

A two-way street

Worcester has long been the industrial heart of central Massachusetts (United States of America). Over the last century and a half, immigrants from Poland, Ireland, Scandinavia and Italy have come to make good in the city's factories. Their children no longer speak the 'old country' language very well. Their children's children are fully integrated Americans.

Such assimilation is unlikely to happen to the latest wave of migrants, who come from Puerto Rico, the Dominican Republic and other Spanish-speaking countries as far away as Ecuador. Most seem to have no intention of giving up either their language or their culture. Indeed, many hope to return home one day.

The recently created Worcester Centro Latino (Spanish Centre) seeks to facilitate the migrants' stay in America. Located in the heart of the Spanish-speaking neighbourhood, the centre offers a variety of services, including literacy and basic education in Spanish and English. Almost any hour during the day or evening, it seems, the centre is buzzing with teaching and learning.

'One pound equals just under half a kilo,' explains a woman in precise English to a semi-circle of newly arrived housewives. In another corner of the centre's storefront headquarters, young men and women are reading two-syllable words in Spanish. Their accents don't sound very Latin: they are Americans learning Spanish.

You ask a staff member of the centre about this class.

'Some people complain that migrants just come to earn as much money as possible and then go away again. But that's not so. We want our presence here to be a two-way street.

'In addition to taking money out of the United States (money we've earned through hard work, by the way), we'd like to bring something of our culture to North Americans. That's why we organize Spanish courses for them here, and also why the centre has helped set up one of the first bilingual public (State) schools in the country.

'Who knows,' the staff member concludes with a wink, 'maybe one day Worcester will become a Spanish city!'

Behind the examples described above stand millions of very real youthful illiterates. The likelihood that they will ever have an opportunity for education is small. But if some of them do have a chance to learn it is thanks in part to the efforts of other young people, who work as teachers and supporters of literacy action, the subjects—respectively—of the next two chapters.

III Youth teaching

Lord Rama's monkeys

G. K. Gaukar is a leader of the literacy drive among Bombay workers
described in the previous chapter. He has a quick smile and an
equally ready stock of colourful stories.

'In the *Ramayana*,' he says, 'Lord Rama wanted to go from India
to Ceylon. Being holy, he could walk across the water. Alas, his
retinue was not endowed with this divine gift. So he called on
helpful monkeys to build a bridge.

'As teachers in our campaign, the educated youth of Bombay are
serving as literacy monkeys.'

The same could be said of almost any literacy programme in the
world today. And no paternalism is intended, for no matter how
noble the inspiration, how ambitious the goal or how modern the
equipment, there is no getting round the need for teachers who
have mental and physical stamina—and will accept little or no pay.
As often as not, young people seem to suit these requirements.

This chapter looks at young people working as literacy teachers in
three ways. First, it presents several categories of young instructors
to show how broad an array of young human resources—from girl
guides to freedom fighters—are actually being mobilized for literacy
teaching. Second, it offers a brief debate between a sceptical and a
protesting point of view, both of which question the suitability of
literacy teaching as an activity for youth. Third, it provides answers
to some of the issues raised during this debate by focusing on two
programmes in which young literacy instructors have played an
important part.

A variety of youthful human resources

Had you followed the Burmese press in the early months of 1971, a succession of headlines might have caught your attention: War on Illiteracy; Move in Campus to Recruit 3-R Teachers; 3-R Instructors Course Opens; Special Trains for University Student Literacy Volunteers; Over 7,200 University Students Helping with 3-R Classes; Illiteracy Wiped out in Mahlaing Township; 95.52 per cent Literate in Meiktila District.

There, in a nutshell, is an example of what university students can accomplish as literacy teachers. It is by no means an isolated case, either. In Mongolia 800 university students have participated in the drive for final liquidation of illiteracy, while Cambodian and Spanish students have also been active, to cite but two other countries.

Predictably, students at teacher-training colleges, and apprentice teachers, have often been active in literacy. Participants from teacher-training institutions in the People's Republic of the Congo and Ethiopia have taught literacy, for instance, while participation of teaching interns in Guatemalan literacy work seems to be widespread.

More surprising, perhaps, is the extent of involvement of secondary-school students in literacy teaching. In fact, the first winner of the Unesco-run Mohammad Reza Pahlavi Prize for meritorious work in literacy was a group of girls at the boarding school in Tabora (Tanzania). Instead of waiting passively for illiterates to come to a community centre, the girls sought them out in their own homes. Another ingenious group of school girls were twenty-five students from the Kasama Girls' Secondary School in northern Zambia. Taking advantage of the enforced immobility of patients at a near-by hospital, they taught literacy to lepers, tuberculosis sufferers and patients in surgical wards with limbs in traction. In Guinea, almost 50,000 secondary-school students received special training in order to work in literacy classes during 1968.

Members of non-student youth organizations of various kinds have also taught literacy in many countries. Under the heading of religious youth bodies, one may point out the literacy activities of the Young Women's Christian Association (YWCA) in India among other places. As for the Youth Catholic Farmers, they have done literacy work in Paraguay, Chad and Cameroon. In the last, a village-level 'school beneath the tree' led to the diversification of family diets, the creation of a small pharmaceutical co-operative (to purchase penicillin more cheaply than through commercial channels) and the construction and repair of wells, springs and roads. Political youth movements form another pool from which literacy teachers have been recruited. The Falcon Movement, an international social democratic youth body, facilitates literacy, for example. In Mongolia, the Revolutionary Union of Youth (REVSOMOL) has—since its creation in 1921—supplied volunteer personnel for literacy work as a means of accomplishing what it views as an 'overriding task . . . the tearing away of the cloud of ignorance'.

Youth groups with an internationalist bent—such as Unesco Clubs in France and Cameroon—have also organized or participated in literacy teaching. In Magadascar, thirty members of an urban Unesco club teach two Sundays a month in a effort to bring literacy to a total of 150 adults in six villages.

Special brigades are another category of young literacy teachers. In Iran, educated conscripts can choose between serving in the army and doing rural development work—including literacy—in one of three special corps. In 1968/69, 8,873 opted for the Education Corps. In addition to running primary schools, they taught literacy to village adults.

Several countries mobilize members of their armed forces for literacy teaching. This is the case with young men in Venezuela and the Dominican Republic—and with girl soldiers in Israel. In that country, 330 women conscripts, all graduates of teacher-training colleges, worked as full-time literacy instructors during 1967/68.

Increasingly recognized is the potential for recruiting young literacy teachers from a hitherto underestimated source: newly literate farmers and workers. In Sodo (Ethiopia), it was found that the newly literate young peasants were more effective than outsiders in teaching illiterate peasants. 'They spoke the same language in more ways than one,' recalls a Unesco expert who was involved in the project.

Last, but not least, in this admittedly incomplete catalogue of various groups of youth who can and do teach literacy come the freedom fighters. Working in liberated areas of countries still under colonial or imperial domination, they link literacy work with the armed struggle. In Angola, for instance, the Movement for the Liberation of Angola (MPLA) militants build the teaching of reading

School-teachers can wield the authority of age, but can young people be taken seriously as literacy instructors?

and writing around key-words of political importance. (This method is similar to the Paolo Freire *concientizaçao* technique, used in some Latin American countries, under which literacy is designed to awaken the conscience of oppressed peasants and workers.)

Literacy teaching—an irrelevant alibi?

Two points of view—opposite to each other, but both critical—look on literacy work as inappropriate, or irrelevant, for youth.

For a start, a sceptic would ask whether young people can really go into literacy instruction seriously enough. It takes years of study and maturation to become a proper school-teacher. Can a bunch of well-meaning teenagers become competent literacy instructors in their off hours? And how do their adult illiterate pupils view them? School-teachers can, at least, wield the authority of age. But the idea of adolescents bringing knowledge to their elders seems ludicrous—particularly in traditional countries, where the older you are the wiser you are thought to become (regardless of whether you can read or write).

Another sceptical point: what is the motivation of these young literacy teachers? However egalitarian their rhetoric may be, are they not really patronizing the poor? Do they not secretly look on themselves as a kind of chivalric élite going to do battle against evil? Are they not presuming rather a lot to act as though they held answers to problems that centuries of efforts have not solved—and that may, in fact, be insoluble?

A protester would attack from another angle, asking: is not literacy ust an irrelevant alibi? It is all very well for youth of industrialized countries to go out to the shanty-towns on a Saturday afternoon and dabble in teaching a few migrant workers to read and write. But would not their efforts be more efficient if they were directed to overthrowing the system that exploits all illiterate foreigners? These literacy instructors may be salving their guilty consciences, a protester would say, but they are not helping the migrants very much.

Answers to these arguments depend very much on the actual situation in which literacy action is taking place with young people's participation. In some places, for example, the argument of irrelevance to real needs is to the point; elsewhere, it may not be. To find some answers in actual situations, let us see how literacy instructors actually look 'on the ground' by focusing on their work in two countries, Madagascar and Cuba.

Close-up and long-view

What follows is not a comparison. Madagascar and Cuba are both tropical island republics with colonial pasts. But, as far as the intention and effect of literacy action and youth's role in it are concerned, they are not comparable. The point here is to show youth teaching in two different situations, and from two points of view. First, this section zooms in for a close-up of the training of members of the Malagasy civic service. Then it dollies back for a long-view of the participation of youth in Cuba's literacy campaign.

Madagascar: focus on training

The headquarters of the Malagasy civic service—under which more and more youths are working for development—is located at the heart of Tananarive, capital of Madagascar.

You go through an arch, and wonder for a second if you're in the right place. In the courtyard, uniformed men bustle around diesel pachyderms whose grunts seem to have a menacing ring. But no; you have not blundered into a military stronghold. The diesel monsters turn out to be peaceful bulldozers under repair. And the uniformed national servicemen are only engaged in what one of their officers tells you is 'a pacific struggle—for development'.

That this pacific struggle is being waged with military seriousness is attested to by the amount and kind of training given to civic service members (about ninety at any given time) who opt to work as village literacy monitors. Out of a total of fourteen months of service, not including three months' military preparation and a one-month leave, civic service literacy volunteers spend months training for a ten-month work period in the countryside. The training includes field-work in addition to classroom lessons in each of four areas.

First, social and economic training. The idea here is to ensure that literacy monitors harness their work to other programmes in the specific socio-economic context of Madagascar. Subjects covered under this heading include: the sociology of the village environment, regional and local development projects, and health protection.

Future monitors are also trained in basic educational statistics, so they will be able quickly and accurately to tabulate marks, calculate averages, rates and percentages, and prepare and comment on tables.

To link literacy to the major concerns of rural communities, trainees receive thorough grounding in agricultural extension work. This is all the more important since many do not come from farming backgrounds. The agricultural training varies, of course, with the crops of the villages to which monitors will be assigned. In paddy areas, for example, great stress is placed on the life-cycle of rice: selection of seeds, choice of ground, transplanting the young shoots, weeding, water control, harvesting, drying, marketing, etc.

All monitors—whatever their assigned area—thoroughly study the Malagasy agricultural vocabulary.

Last, and probably most important, is educational training. Here, an examination of adult psychology and its consequences for the educator serves as a foundation for introducing work with the selective, work-oriented and functional approach to literacy. Since Madagascar is participating in Unesco's Experimental World Literacy Programme, special emphasis is given to training in the new approach.

For example, trainees are taught how to base the subjects of language and reading on a study of the everyday environment. And the same orientation permeates training in the conception, production, use and evaluation of flannelgraphs, posters and audio-visual media, and in the preparation of a teaching schedule based on the agricultural calendar.

A sceptic might ask if all this training is really necessary. Instruction in literacy teaching, he would concede, is indispensable. But what about some of the other topics, so peripheral to reading and writing as to be barely on—if not beyond—the horizon of the working literacy monitor. Lessons about 'the sociology of the village environment', for example, may be interesting—but how really vital are they to the teaching of the three R's?

Very vital indeed, one civic serviceman would answer. Assigned to a particularly isolated village, he made good progress in getting literacy classes under way. Then, one day early in 1969, Hurricane Dany devastated the region. Destruction of houses and fields was widespread. But the monitor in question found that his friendly relations with the villagers had also disintegrated in the wake of the storm—despite the fact that, during it, he had dived into a river to save the life of a drowning village child.

Without training in village-level sociology, he might well not have analysed the worsening relationships coolly and rationally. And he almost certainly wouldn't have found out that the villagers were convinced that he—the only outsider for miles around—had put a hex on them and caused the cyclone!

National leaders of the Madagascar literacy programme, and Unesco advisers working with them, generally believe that only through exhaustive training can the civic service literacy monitors be assured a good chance of success. Are they successful? Monitors must be doing something right when, after several months (that is, after the novelty has worn off), villagers continue to sacrifice several evenings a week to learning. In many cases, the attendance rate remains as high as 95 per cent.

Local popularity is only one criterion of success, would come the sceptic's rejoinder. What about assessing the civic service literacy monitors by other criteria, the economic criterion, for instance? Is it sound economics to invest in four months of training for only ten months of work?

The work of most civic servicemen involved in literacy does not, in fact, end with their mustering out from national service. Quite the contrary; they are signed on as full-time professionals by the Malagasy Government. So the investment is in a career, not just ten months.

Cuba: a success story with no end

Between 1 January and 31 December 1961 the number of illiterates among adults in Cuba was reduced from 23.6 per cent to 3.9 per cent.

This was not an act of God, a magic trick or the result of an epidemic that struck only those who could not read and write. It was a success achieved by the direct, permanent, long-term and personal involvement of 15 per cent of the entire population: some 700,000 illiterates plus 271,000 literacy workers—mostly unpaid, part-time and full-time volunteers.

It must be said that illiteracy in Cuba was not so severe a problem as in some Third World countries: First of all, three-quarters of the adult population was already literate at the start of the campaign, while the number often quoted as a minimum for development 'take-off' is between 30 per cent and 40 per cent. Then, communications were not so difficult—in many parts of the island, at least—as they often are in developing countries. Third, because of bad organization before the Revolution, a number of qualified teachers and educational administrators were actually unemployed.

Whatever advantages it had, Cuba's effort can only be described as remarkable.

The role of young instructors in reaching the goal of complete literacy has been called a 'decisive factor' by the Cuban Ministry of Education. From the planning stage on, youth organizations worked side by side with adult institutions on the National Literacy Commission, which was responsible for mounting, co-ordinating and evaluating the campaign.

Indeed, youth volunteered *en masse* for literacy instruction brigades. The majority of the youthful contingent came off the school-benches. Educational establishments closed on 15 April 1961—several weeks earlier than usual—in order to enable pupils and students to take part. A week later, 7,220 youngsters were already undergoing training. Another week, and their number had almost doubled. It continued to swell, even after the first trainees left to start literacy teaching. The training camp (located not far from Havana) closed on 31 August. By then, 105,664 young people had become *brigadistas*.

And they were truly young. Almost twice as many came from primary school as from secondary. An 18-year-old felt decidedly elderly in their midst as the average age was between 14 and 16. Cynics might have cracked doubting jokes about this twentieth-century children's crusade, but they were quickly silenced by results.

Equipped with hammocks, lanterns and specially produced adult primers, the *brigadistas* fanned out into the countryside, where most Cubans then lived—and where the illiteracy rate was twice the national average.

Wherever they went, they set to work at once motivating the people to learn, teaching them, testing their progress and tabulating the results for inclusion in national statistics.

It would have been unreasonable to expect such a mass mobilization to happen without a hitch and there were numerous problems. Transporting people, books and supplies to the right places at the right times caused the organizers many headaches. Feeding and caring for volunteers in desolate localities where illiteracy was synonymous with undernourishment and ill health was not easy either. Also, there were unavoidable misunderstandings between *brigadistas*, who were generally of fairly educated town backgrounds, and unlettered rural people.

These misunderstandings, however, were a source of learning on both sides. This showed that, in literacy work using young teachers, the education can be mutual.

Many *brigadistas* previously had no idea how the 'other half' lived, or what it thought, feared and desired. Through daily working contacts with farm people, they came to realize, how very desperate the situation of the peasantry was. Many resolved to choose careers that would help improve the lot of Cuba's majority. Seventy per cent of them received scholarships for further study in fields essential to development, often education.

Today, a decade later, a healthy percentage of the country's educational personnel is made up of brigade veterans. There are numerous teachers and even headmasters of 25 or 26 for whom participation in the campaign was a vocational and personal turning point. Through it, they learned a kind of literacy in social awareness.

Does the success story of the 1961 campaign in Cuba sound too good to be true? Perhaps it would, if it ended here. But it doesn't.

Undergoing what it called 'our own apprenticeship', the Cuban leadership decided that the conclusion of the campaign marked a beginning, not an end. The three R's were not considered a widely useful minimum in a society embarking on rapid economic growth and deep social change. The threshold of mass education was raised. A person would only be considered really literate once he or she had completed a 'follow-up' course, the earliest of which graduated its first pupils in December 1962.

In the years since, the threshold has been raised again, more than once. From 'follow-up' courses it moved through the 'technical minimum' to the 'battle for the sixth grade'. In a sense, and despite the many obstacles encountered, this periodic raising of literacy sights in Cuba is a success story that has no end.

It is all very well (you may be thinking) to talk about young people who have the time to devote several hours a week to literacy teaching, or to serve full-time as instructors for several months or a year or even longer. But what about those who do not have that kind of free time? And those whose gifts do not lie in the teaching field? And those who live in communities where illiteracy is not a problem?

What can they do about literacy? The next chapter offers some answers.

IV Youth supporting

In any army in the world, there are about ten people at the rear for every soldier on the front lines. So, with literacy, the battle would be hopeless if instructors (and learners) were left without moral and logistic support of various kinds. For example, reading primers appropriate for adults of a given country—or even of a given region, social stratum and occupation within that country—must be designed written, illustrated, tested, printed and distributed.

Although possibly less glamorous than actual instruction, behind-the-lines support activities have mobilized many young people interested in literacy in all parts of the world. Generally speaking, and while some activities are interchangeable, support action takes place at three levels: developing countries, industrialized countries, and joint efforts.

This chapter looks at youth's participation in literacy support activities—sometimes routine, sometimes ingenious—at each of these levels in turn.

In developing countries: from promotion to follow-up

If we take support activities carried out by youth in Third World countries in order of the schedule governing any literacy programme, we come first to promotion. This is a conveniently vague Latin-root word that, translated into down-to-earth Anglo-Saxon, means 'getting things going'. Linked to literacy, it involves forming and informing various sectors of public opinion—and public opinion as a whole—so as to create an atmosphere favourable to intensified action. For a member of the Youth Rights Department of the World Federation of Democratic Youth, mobilization of public opinion is

A behind-the-lines force in the battle for literacy.

'obviously the key to success for campaigns against illiteracy'. In order to motivate illiterates, the girl guides of Kenya organized demonstrations at rural market places and community development centres to incite housewives to join the country's Women's Association, which gives literacy courses. The annual observance of International Literacy Day (8 September) provides a handy hook on which promotion can be hung. One year, the United Towns Organization issued an appeal on literacy to some 850 national and local committees in 51 countries.

Fund-raising for literacy, although less widespread than in industrialized countries, has been carried out by Third World young people. In 1965, members of Calcutta University created the West Bengal Students' Council to Eradicate Illiteracy. According to one report, 'They did not lack in sincerity, but they lacked funds'. The streets of Calcutta are not exactly paved with gold, and the students cast about in search of a way to raise money. 'What resource have we?' they asked. The answer they finally hit on was their own blood, which they sold to get their work under way.

Preparation for literacy courses covers a number of supporting activities. In Madagascar, Unesco clubs linked to secondary schools and the university put on a benefit performance to raise funds for the construction of cultural centres actually to be built by club members in the framework of Unesco's Experimental Literacy Project in that country. In Jamaica, the Girl Guides Association also fitted out a centre for literacy and other adult-education activities.

The gathering of statistics for literacy work is another activity with which young people are helping. In the early 1960s, members of the REVSOMOL organization took part in a survey to determine the amount of illiteracy and semi-literacy remaining in Mongolia.

The Ethiopian University Service—a programme under which all students at Haile Selassie I University in Addis Ababa serve a year doing development-related tasks in the countryside—has also taken part in the preparation, testing and evaluation of audio-visual materials to be used in connexion with literacy instruction. It is not sufficient for media experts sitting in capital cities to think up attractive ideas for films, slides, radio programmes and the like. If they are not tested before wide distribution, they can (and often do) prove so foreign to the experience and understanding of illiterates as to be useless, or even harmful.

During the actual running of literacy drives, Third World young people have served as intermediaries between literacy instructors on the one hand, and literacy organizers, on the other. In Ethiopia again, University Service participants serve as itinerant supervisors. Their tasks include encouraging teachers, writing reports, keeping tabs on finance, etc. This sort of administrative routine may not be very exciting, but it must be carried out if programmes are to function with anything approaching smoothness.

We have already seen that literacy work which stops with the basic three R's generally useless and soon forgotten. Follow-up is indispensable—and here, too, young people have been active.

A recent inquiry among successful graduates of a literacy course in one African town revealed that less than 10 per cent could read and write without great difficulty. Further education for new literates which is carried out with youth participation takes many forms, and is not limited to classical classroom work. Thus, several hundred Spanish students volunteer each summer under the University Work Service Scheme to organize informal cultural activities directed at new literates in rural areas.

Establishing and improving libraries and ensuring their use, are other follow-up measures in which young people are becoming increasingly involved. The Peruvian Girl Guides Association is opening a library-cum-recreation centre for new literates, for example.

Producing reading material to put into the libraries, and to distribute in general to new literates, is another follow-up area that has attracted young people. In Ethiopia, girl students in the University Service have written home-economics texts, while a boy—also working under the service—edited a special magazine for students and graduates of literacy courses.

In industrialized countries: help for literacy near and far

Action in support of literacy by young people in industrialized countries centres on two goals: helping literacy at home and aiding literacy in the Third World.

Supporting activities for programmes at home follow more or less the same pattern reported in the previous section for developing countries. In France, for instance, young people and youth organizations concerned with illiteracy among migrants joined other groups in forming a Liaison Committee for Literacy and Promotion, one of whose functions it to arouse public opinion and further governmental and private action on the problem.

Some young people have also found it suitable to serve as tutors with migrants' children who run into difficulties with their schoolwork. Volunteers from the Unesco Club at Bois-Colombes, a suburb of Paris, work an hour each week with Algerian and Portuguese pupils from a local school, for example.

More often than not, it is literacy in the Third World rather than at home that has sparked the initiative of youth in industrialized countries. Generally, the initiative is directed first at fact finding.

Youth organizations with an international bent (such as Unesco Clubs and United Nations student associations) have, now and again in the past, made efforts to learn about the world illiteracy problem. Of late, however, there are indications that interest in the issue is creeping through the walls that separate out-of-school activities from the in-school curriculum.

At the University of Massachusetts School of Education (United States), for example, illiteracy and literacy are covered in an introductory course on international education. In this course, graduates and undergraduates take part in a simulation exercise called the 'International Conference Game' at which they play the part of Third World education ministers who must share out a specified budget among several educational priorities (including literacy) in a limited amount of time. In a more academic vein, an eight member student study group at Vincennes (France) spent the first semester of the 1970/71 year preparing a report comparing the Paolo Freire 'conscientization' literacy method with the Unesco selective functional and work-oriented approach.

To date, the major effort of industrialized youth in support of Third World literacy has been spent in collecting and sending material resources. In some cases, these have been transferred in kind. Thus, the International Union of Students and the International Student Conference provided typewriters, posters and other equipment and materials for literacy work carried out under the auspices of the Chilean National Union of Students.

Most often, resource transfers take the form of fund-raising campaigns. Young people and their organizations in industrialized countries have displayed considerable ingenuity in devising ways of 'getting through' to the even-more solicited—and therefore ever more *blasé*—audience of potential donors.

In the framework of the Unesco Gift Coupon Programme a travelling campaign is being carried out by students from Winnipeg (Canada) at this writing. Touring their home country and the United States by special bus, they are giving shows of various kinds to raise money for literacy in Latin America—money that they hope to deliver in person.

Another imaginative means of collecting funds for literacy and adult education has been used by Swedish university students. In 1969, 49 per cent of them paid a voluntary tax, of whose proceeds 27 per cent went to the educational programmes of the Mozambique Liberation Front, FRELIMO.

No matter how ingenious, however, fund-collecting is increasingly thought to raise almost as many problems as it solves, if not more. This is the feeling of a *Guide for Student Action in Development* produced by a joint study group convened by the World University Service and the International Student Movement for the United Nations with the help of the Food and Agriculture Organization's Freedom from Hunger Campaign.

The *Guide* asks if fund-raising is based on the simplistic notion that a mere transfer of resources from rich countries to poor is sufficient to promote development. Do citizens of the rich countries drop a few coins of conscience money in the annual collection box—and then forget about the Third World until the next year? If so, says the *Guide,* fund-raising does not 'get to the heart of the problem; and if it is done in such a way as to perpetuate false notions, i.e. that it [fund-raising] is sufficient in itself, it can lead to further misunderstanding and delay proper action'.

The nectar of ideas and half a million kroner

'Proper action' clearly implies political action; and an important underpinning of effective political action is mass awareness. Collecting money and spreading information were the twin goals of a nation-wide campaign organized by Danish secondary-school students in 1969. The campaign—called *Operation Dagsværk* (Operation Day's Work (OD))—is important enough to describe in some detail both because of the ways it succeeded and on account of where, how and why it failed.

'In a castle of thought lives the happy student,' goes an old Danish university ditty, 'and he sups on the nectar of ideas.' Danish students may once have been more prone to theory than practice. But this no longer seems to be the case. Operation Day's Work is proof of the change.

In 1967/68 a politically minded generation gained control of Denmark's Secondary School Student Association. The new leadership noted the success of its counterparts in other Scandinavian countries in raising funds for development work by getting students to turn over salaries earned during one day's work each year. The association's General Assembly decided that the 30,000 Danish secondary-school students should also contribute to the Third World—while learning about it and bringing development issues home to the general public—through the Day's Work technique.

To focus their efforts as much as possible, in public information as well as fund-allocation, the association's leaders decided to find one project in one developing country. In search of such a project, they wrote to Unesco.

Unesco replied with a portfolio of seven possibilities. A copy of this portfolio was sent to the student council at each of Denmark's 100 gymnasiums (classical secondary schools).

'By sending the files round to all schools we were not only following democratic procedure,' recalls Torben Brylle, who looks like a fair-haired bear with spectacles and was one of the Day's Work organizers. 'We were also trying to initiate the information activities from the outset. We wanted to get students to find out about the countries Unesco was suggesting. And we wanted them to learn about the problems and methods of development involved in the different projects.'

Time was fleeting. It was already 1969. If the intention to hold a campaign during the following school year was to be carried out, a decision would have to be taken soon. So, in February 1969, the Danish Secondary School Student Association, in conjunction with a similar body in Norway, selected Unesco's Experimental World Literacy Project in Zambia.

'From then on,' laughs Torben Brylle, 'the five of us who were assigned to mount Operation Day's Work stopped getting enough sleep.

'It was as though we'd been put in charge of a rocket launching at Cape Kennedy or Baikonur. There were so many things to do ourselves, and so many other people to get cracking on different parts of the project, and such a great need to see that the things we did and the parts others were working on all meshed together precisely on schedule. . . .

First came the schedule itself. The operation was to last a week during which individuals and groups would be released from school for one day on condition that they do some kind of job and contribute their earnings to Zambia through OD. But when should that week take place?

Not in the spring—too many students would be preparing exams Nor in the winter—outdoor jobs would not be available. The autumn, then? Though only a few months away, the autumn seemed the most convenient time—or, rather, the least inconvenient time Day's Work would take place between 3 and 11 October.

Next decision? The target sum of money to be raised.

'Here we operated almost by guess work,' says Torben.

'We'd look foolhardy if we set too ambitious a target, and conservative if we didn't aim high enough. We considered extreme proposals—from 1 million kroner to 100,000 kroner—then split the difference.'

The Danish Day's Work would try to raise 500,000 kroner— U.S.$67,000.

O K. Next decision?

'It wasn't decisions but actions that were necessary. The school year was almost over and we had to get organized before our manpower drifted away for the summer.'

First, every school was encouraged to set up a Day's Work action committee. Each committee, it was suggested, should have work groups to deal with publicity; co-operation with the local authorities co-operation with employers and trade unions; co-operation with community organizations; finance; and so on.

Then came contacts between the OD organizers in Copenhagen and the government and national organizations of various kinds

The Night School Pupils Organization—made up mostly of secondary-school-age working youth—joined the Secondary School Student Association in sponsoring the project. The Ministry of Finance readily granted permission to export 'a large sum of money in hard currency. ('We certainly hoped it was going to be a ''large sum of money'',' comments Torben.) The Ministry of Education authorized gymnasium headmasters throughout the country to grant students a day off during OD week—on condition that they present proof of doing a Day's Work job. ('That was pretty heavy pressure in our favour,' Torben admits. 'But no one was actually preventing students from staying in school if they wanted to.') The employers' organization expressed interest in the project. After initial hesitation because they thought students might be taking much needed jobs in areas of high regional unemployment, the trade unions also gave a green light. ('They urged us not to let people accept salaries lower than the minimum wage. "No fear of that!" we told them.')

When school let out for the summer, Torben and his fellow organizers surveyed their accomplishments with satisfaction. The different components of their 'rocket launch' were being put together more or less smoothly.

'Then we thought,"My God! 3 October is only three months away!"'

During the summer they concentrated on three tasks. The first was contacts with the press. 'The journalists were very hard-headed,' recalls Torben. 'They wanted action, not just a lot of words. And we didn't have much action to give them—not yet.'

Second, 'Job offers were not flooding our mailbox, so we had to go out and beat the bushes'. This involved criss-crossing Denmark to visit potential employers of Day's Work volunteers. 'Some firms were quite co-operative. Others turned us down. They said that development aid should be given by the government, and that's why they pay taxes, and so on. When we explained that much official development aid comes right back to the industries of "donor" countries and isn't really a gift at all; they stopped listening.

While Torben and his friends were out 'beating the bushes', their colleagues in Norway were also trying to find jobs, by offering services to individuals as well as institutions. 'We'll come by nice and early to wake you up,' began one Norwegian brochure. 'We'll give you coffee in bed. We'll take your dog for his morning walk. We'll type your letters. We'll paint your house. We'll wash your car. We'll wash your windows. We'll wash you ... We'll do your marketing . . . We'll serve you dinner . . . We'll play the piano for you . . . We'll wish you good night.'

The third summer task for the Danish OD organizers was to prepare information materials about literacy, Zambia, and literacy in Zambia. They brain-stormed with university people, journalists, government officials and other specialists. Although Unesco itself was not equipped to supply large quantities of detailed information o n all aspects of the Zambia project, the Danish National Commission for Unesco did finance the publication of a short folder. A special supplement to *Gymnasiebladet,* the national secondary-school student newspaper, was also prepared.

When gymnasiums opened for the 1969/70 school year, their students were submerged in what Torben calls 'a tidal wave of Day's Work propaganda'.

With a month to go until 3 October, the 'countdown' began. Now it was absolutely essential to get timing and priorities just right. The organizers took stock—at least tried to.

'We had some idea of what we'd started, but we didn't know how far it had gone.'

A quick straw poll showed that there were not yet nearly enough student volunteers or jobs to reach the half-million kroner mark. To ensure more local initiative, rather than have lines of communication only with the capital, the OD structure was divided into a dozen regions. Publicity was also intensified, thanks to stepped-up schedules of meetings, rallies and film-showings. A special effort was made in Copenhagen, which—as a cosmopolitan city—was more impervious to the mounting excitement of campaign preparations than the rest of the country.

For Torben, 2 October, the eve of the first day of OD week, 'was just awful'. It was cold and raining. One school director had just decided to send all his students off for seven days' practical training instead of letting them do Day's Work. 'Even though we'd got into the news, it was bad news: one newspaper was predicting ''a fiasco''.'

'It was too late to do anything more about it. The third of October was only the first of seven OD days. But we knew it would give us a good idea of whether the students would end up heroes or fools. It was going to be like that agonizing moment after the count-down has reached zero, when flames are shooting out of the tail of the rocket, but before the rocket itself actually begins to rise.'

Success, failure and one happy elephant

At 6 a.m. on 3 October, Torben climbed out of a sleeping bag at the student association's headquarters, high under the eaves of a building in an old part of Copenhagen. Ten minutes later he was

One way of earning money for literacy—it's been tried.

on his way to Rødovre, a suburb, where a printer had finished a rush OD brochure job late the previous night.

'Usually the man had a beer and a joke ready for me when I came by to pick up finished work. But that morning he was as sober and solemn as a judge—I think he was as worried about Day's Work as we were. By way of wishing us good luck, he said he'd hired an OD student for the day.'

By 8 a.m., having delivered all the new brochures, Torben was back at headquarters.

'Phones were ringing like mad and all sorts of people were milling in to answer a last-minute radio appeal for more jobs in Copenhagen.'

At 8.30 a.m. Torben wandered down the Strøget, a mile-long, shop-lined pedestrian street running through the centre of the city.

'A few dozen of our people were out, ready to shine shoes. But there was a cold wind blowing and not many passers-by were stopping to take advantage of their services.

Between 8.45 and 9.30 a.m., he visited a few firms to arrange student placement on the way to the office of a newspaper that had not given the project very good coverage.

'At the newspaper a reporter told me we'd only hit the front page if we had something "spectacular".' 'Like what?', I asked him. 'Oh, let's say a pretty girl washing an elephant.'

'It was against our better judgement, since we were trying to inform the public, not sell them merchandise; but we went ahead and arranged for a pretty girl to wash an elephant at the zoo. That made thirty kroner for literacy, one happy journalist, and maybe one happy elephant.'

Passing though the Strøget again at 11.30 a.m., Torben found OD shoe-shines selling like hot cakes among the lunch-time crowd. On a near-by street corner, he also spied two Day's Work boys lounging in deck-chairs.

'I got a little cross, and went over to tell them to get back to work. But it turned out they were working—counting cars for the city traffic department!'

By noon, calls reporting on jobs under way or already done were beginning to outnumber requests for work or workers at the student association's headquarters. Even the organizers were surprised by the diversity of things students all over the country had found to do.

In northern Zealand, girls baked a mountain of cakes, which they sold on the town square. In Vejle, there was an auction of African handicrafts. In Grena, a student band played in the streets. Apples were picked in Glamsbjerg. Jutland actors put on a benefit. Newspapers in Copenhagen bought articles and drawings. Elsewhere, students painted houses, collected refuse and worked as wrappers in stores, to mention just three other jobs.

Seven days later, newspaper headlines reported the results. 'Elsinore Highschool Students Net 11,357 Kroner!', went one. And another: 'Fine Result for OD—3,500 Kroner Earned Locally Will Go to Unesco.' Said a third: '15,500 Kroner from Viborg to Zambia!' In the town where one paper had predicted a fiasco, its competitor took malicious pleasure in declaring Day's Work 'A Great Success!'

Seen from the perspective of hindsight, was it really a success?

'Well, we did reach the fund-raising target,' says Torben Brylle. 'In fact, we raised about 540,000 kroner in all. Also, we mobilized a lot of students, in Danish terms at least. About 20,000 went out and did a day's work—that's roughly two-thirds of the secondary-school student population.

'On the other hand, as for the equally important goal of informing people about underdevelopment, literacy and Zambia .... Well, I honestly don't think we achieved very much at all. Some of the students did want to do something for the Third World, in a vague kind of way. But most went along with the project because it was fun and "the thing to do", or quite simply because they got a day off from school.

'There were exceptions, of course, but they were already interested and informed before we began—and the circle of interested and informed students didn't grow very much as a result of Day's Work.'

Torben is equally pessimistic about the impact of the operation on public opinion at large. 'Despite pretty good newspaper coverage most people didn't learn anything about Zambia or literacy. For public opinion, OD was some kind of charity affair.'

A recent visitor to Copenhagen found confirmation of Torben's appraisal in the reaction of one taxi-driver, at least:

'*Dagsværk?* Oh yes, I remember it very well. It was a bunch of hippies raising money for poor people in, er, France, I think.'

Joint action: the problem of distance

Having seen what young people in developing countries and industrialized countries are doing separately, we can end this chapter on youth supporting literacy action by asking what they are doing together. The answer is: not very much. Bridging the physical distance is, still, too expensive for joint literacy action to be very widespread.

There have, of course, been international meetings on the subject in which young people and youth organizations have participated— or for which they have been responsible. Youth associations and movements from the industrialized as well as the developing countries took an active part in the organization and work of African, Asian and Latin American regional seminars of literacy held by international non-governmental organizations in the framework of their co-operation with Unesco. One, in fact, was organized by the World Assembly of Youth.

With due respect to such gatherings—exchanging ideas and information or fixing targets and programmes of future action— these justify themselves to protester and sceptic alike only when they lead to concrete action.

International service by youth is one example of such action. For a number of years, international voluntary work-camps in many Third World countries have enabled young people from around the world to build community development centres and literacy centres, and do other jobs directly or indirectly facilitating literacy programmes.

In the last decade, furthermore, volunteer technicians have gone by the thousands from Europe and North America to Asia, Africa and Latin America to work for a year or two in their speciality. In some cases, their jobs have had a direct relation to literacy.

An international group of volunteers worked with the staff of Unesco's Experimental Literacy Project in Tanzania. In addition to a Danish administrator and two American Quakers, a team of seven young Finns worked in various capacities. Two served as secretaries, another as a graphic artist and a fourth as an agricultural mechanic. There was also a building worker, a printer and a correspondent. The correspondent, a young woman, later became engaged to a Tanzanian and returned to the country. She continued to supply a flow of feature articles, radio interviews and other news on the project to Finland, where money was being raised for literacy work in Tanzania.

In this chapter, and the two that preceded it, we have looked at what young people are doing today in the field of literacy. How can their work be evaluated? And what are the prospects for future involvement of young people in literacy action? These questions are covered—briefly—in the next chapter.

V   What next?

Let's be quite frank. In world terms, young people's participation in literacy as learners, teachers and supporters has worked, and is working, no miracles.

If we focus on the teaching and supporting roles—those which readers of this booklet might want to play—we see that in some villages and cities, and in a very few countries, youth has been a decisive factor for literacy. But the general picture is much bleaker.

Compared to the total population of potential young teachers and supporters, only a handful are actually involved. And their involvement is generally in micro-projects that are scattered and isolated, without sufficient continuity or relation to national efforts—which themselves are often absent.

Symbolic pilot activities are important, of course. But experimentation alone is simply not enough. As a Unesco official recently told the author apropos of youth's current involvement in literacy, 'there's only one chance in a million that you'll blow up the lab by fooling around with the contents of a single test-tube'.

Meanwhile, there is a growing impatience in the world to get on with more massive and more effective literacy work. Clearly, young people are a resource that could be mobilized in much greater numbers than now and in much better programmes to make literacy more massive and effective. It may be that literacy can only become more massive and effective if youth is so mobilized. How might this come about?

Without making any hard-and-fast predictions, a glance at the crystal ball yields some fascinating projections of things to come.

It shows, simultaneously with the growing impatience for adult literacy (and development as a whole), a spreading dissatisfaction with schooling of youth that is cut off from real life, that is increasingly called irrelevant. It takes only the simplest futuristic calculation to put one and one together—and get a new educational system which would link youth's desire for relevant education with the need for middle-level development workers, including teachers and supporters of literacy.

There are already isolated cases where spare-time or full-time participation of youth in literacy and other forms of development service is viewed as an educationally beneficial alternative to classroom exercises. In some instances, such 'experiential learning' receives academic sanction. In a few, it is a required part of one's education. The Ethiopian University Service, already described above, is an example here. Another is the system under which students in Guatemala who run literacy classes receive points that count toward their final examination grade, with student-teachers being expected to make six people literate before they can graduate.

Not all such programmes work smoothly, of course. Often, problems stem from the fact that the service period is not considered or treated as an organic part of the student's education. He or she is insufficiently prepared for a given job in a given place beforehand, and receives little or no help in integrating the work into his or her total educational experience afterwards.

But most problems could be ironed out, and those remaining would not seriously diminish the multiple advantages that could be derived from a generalized serve-and-learn option, if not obligation.

Psychologically, the widespread present-day student frustration at being of, but not in, the world would be reduced. Educationally, the opportunity to complement classroom theory with practical first-hand knowledge would be greatly expanded. Economically, the world's investment in education would begin to pay off much sooner than at present—and at a higher rate, since students would not receive full salaries. And, in terms of development, a service-cum-education scheme would vastly increase the pool of manpower available for literacy work and other tasks promoting economic growth and social change.

What would such a system look like? Each country would have its own variant, of course. But there would also be some common features.

In the Third World, students from upper-primary classes straight through university would be offered the possibility of undertaking

What can I do? Chapter VI gives some of the answers.

development activities instead of classroom work during a period or periods (part-time or full-time) of their educational career. Those mobilized to teach literacy might often come from teacher-training institutions. Those working to support literacy would come from a variety of educational backgrounds: vocational schools would supply printers, secretaries, etc. Instead of writing compositions on the seventeenth-century theatre, English students could work (in teams, perhaps) on material for new literates. And so on.

In industrialized countries, students would be seconded both for literacy work with migrants and for action in support of literacy in the Third World. Classes in schools of commerce and administration might organize fund-raising campaigns, for example.

It would be vitally important to ensure that such work stints were integrated into students' over-all education. This implies a necessary—and healthy— reorientation of at least part of existing curricula so as to prepare students for actual jobs, and to help them analyse the results of the work once they have finished their service period(s). As to finance, it seems very likely that costs of administering such a scheme would be more than offset by two factors. First, students on their work assignments would not be using school facilities or teachers—whence reduced expenditure by the educational system. Second, they would be making a contribution of measurable value through their work.

Sceptics and protesters would doubtless criticize such a system. A sceptic would say that it is not fair to coerce—or even put social pressure on—students to turn them into temporary cheap labour. This was precisely the objection of university students in one Third World country who went on strike when a student service scheme was introduced. To many observers, the government's reply— dismissal of all students who refused service—was far from unjustified.

The government's argument was that in democratic countries there is no place for a privileged élite, and that in poor countries an unproductive student minority is all the more intolerable since it owes its education to the hard work of the impoverished majority. Far from enjoying special rights, the government said, the educated few have extra duties toward the majority that made their education possible. Service is one way to begin paying that debt.

A protester would probably say that the serve-and-learn idea is just one more way of co-opting youth's critical thinking and rebellious energies in order to make them work for the Establishment. In some instances, this may be so. But other cases suggest that, far from neutralizing young people, service tends to radicalize them by putting them into daily contact—often for the first time in their lives—with the reality of illiteracy, ill health and so on.

You may have noticed that, as we approach the conclusion of this little book, the sceptic has remained sceptical and the protester is still protesting. This was to be expected. Any other outcome would be a fairytale ending—all too common in institutional writing. It would be as though we were living happily ever after in a world with no problems (and, therefore, no illiteracy), without dissension (and, therefore, without progress).

But where do you stand?

With regard to literacy action today, and youth's role in it, are you a sceptic? A protester? Something else?

If you are a sceptic, you might just as well stop reading now; the next chapter's suggested activities will not interest you.

If, on the other hand, you are a protester or someone who is even only mildly concerned by the world illiteracy problem, you may be asking 'What can I do?' If that question is in your mind, please turn the page.

VI What you can do: 'imagination takes over'[1]

Illiteracy is huge, complex, intractable and persistent. To overcome illiteracy is going to require that more people than now do harder work—and, equally important, that they do more imaginative work.

More imaginative work means giving your own blood to raise funds, like the students of Calcutta, rather than throwing up your hands and saying 'there's no money'. It means mobilizing the very young as literacy teachers, as in Cuba, rather than saying only adults or near-adults can teach adults. It means not being afraid to question what you are doing about literacy, or what anybody else is doing, just as Unesco has printed in this booklet a sceptic's and a protester's critique of its literacy approach and work. And imagination means having the nerve, or cheek (or whatever it is) to declare, with the American Freedom from Hunger Young World Development Group, that 'some of us had better choose to define ourselves as world problem solvers'.

Let us review some of the categories of youth action for literacy to which an imaginative approach could be applied.

The first question you might ask is whether you want to do anything, directly, about literacy. It may be that in your country, or your community, the long-term goal of literacy would best be served by action in other fields first.

Perhaps you might want to begin with a call for more funds for education in general, either in your nation's budget, if you live in a developing country, or in its foreign-aid programmes, if you are the citizen of an industrialized country. If illiteracy among migrants is a problem in your community, perhaps it would be best to start with a campaign against racism and substandard working and living conditions. If you are concerned about illiteracy as part and

1. *Source:* Anonymous authors of graffiti at the University of Paris (France).

parcel of the underdevelopment of the Third World, a good focal point for action might be to find out whether existing international trade and economic relations are helping or hurting the poor countries.

Action directly linked to literacy might come under one or more of the following four headings, or any combination of them.

First, you can find out more about illiteracy and literacy. What are the facts, figures and trends of illiteracy and literacy in the world? In your own community? How do you, personally, judge illiteracy? By moral criteria ('It's a scandal'), by political criteria ('It's unjust'), by socio-economic criteria ('It prevents development'), or by other criteria?[1]

What is being done in your community or country to fight illiteracy? What action is being taken in other countries? Internationally? Are all these efforts effective? If not, why not?

Finding out more about illiteracy can be an individual or group project. You might want to read up in your spare time, or for a course in school. Or, like one student at the University of Rome, you might want to do a doctorate on the subject.

Second, you can try to influence public opinion. There are standard ways of doing this: writing to the press, contacting legislators, alerting radio and television, setting up displays, opening special libraries, sticking posters and the like. And there are less-standard ways: guerrilla theatre, demonstrations .... A joint study group of the World University Service (WUS) and International Student Movement for the United Nations (ISMUN) on student action for development has even suggested that, if all else fails, civil disobedience may be considered. Exactly how far it is appropriate to escalate action depends on many circumstances. And each situation should be carefully analysed before the kind and intensity of activity is determined. In some cases, a dramatic presentation of the facts will suffice. Elsewhere, or at another time, it may prove necessary (in the opinion of the WUS-ISMUN study group) to strive to 'make people . . . angry at the existence of social and economic imbalance . . .'.

When trying to form and inform public opinion, consider what organizational channels you want to use. Perhaps new associations

---

1. Reading that would be useful for fact-finding is suggested at the end of this book.

need to be formed—like the Youth D-Groups (Development Groups) that are springing up throughout Scandinavia. Alternatively, a fresh look at existing bodies may reveal unsuspected opportunities. Do trade unions in industrialized countries seem more concerned with bread and butter at home than with illiteracy and under-development abroad? Do religious institutions appear other-worldly? Do political parties come across as blind to the woods of planetary problems because of their preoccupation with the trees of the next elections?

And what about clubs, associations and movements of young people? What role—if any— should they play in literacy?

Appropriate action can achieve results, sometimes swift and radical results. The last few years have shown that, in many countries, student pressure can make school curricula more relevant, for example. (By the way, did or does your school cover illiteracy in any of its courses?)

Third, you can raise money for literacy work. Operation Day's Work showed that ingenious (and humorous) projects can reap as good a harvest as simply passing the hat, if not better. It also demonstrated that the public information side of fund-raising, although necessary, is extremely difficult to run effectively. What projects can you think of that would be as successful in presenting facts and ideas about illiteracy as in bringing in money for literacy?[1]

Finally, you can take part in the actual organization of literacy work. You can teach, keeping in mind the need for previous training. And you can undertake support activities, with the realization that they are sometimes the key to success of a literacy programme. Opening a day-care centre may be the only way to let illiterate mothers attend classes. Rejuvenating a library may prove indis-pensable in preventing new literates from forgetting how to read and write.[2]

1. If you wish to contribute to literacy abroad, keep in mind the possibility of transferring funds through the Unesco Gift Coupon Programme to carefully vetted projects with which you can enter into direct contact. The address is: Gift Coupon Office, Unesco, Place de Fontenoy, 75 Paris-7e (France).
2. If you want to volunteer for service abroad in connexion with literacy work, write to: Co-ordinating Committee for International Voluntary Service, 1 Rue Miollis, 75 Paris-15e (France), for information. Please be sure to enclose two International Reply Coupons obtainable at post offices.

A little help from their friends

The Beatles used to claim that one can get by with a little help from one's friends. What about the people who cannot read or write—will they get by, even with a lot of help? The answer is uncertain.

The number of illiterate adults is growing each year. And each year, the number of children reaching adolescence without knowing how to read and write is greater than the number of adults who have become literate. So the total eradication of illiteracy would seem to be retreating toward the horizon. Is pessimism, then, the only realistic attitude? Perhaps not—not if one keeps in mind that illiteracy might be wiped out with the cost of a single moon shot.

Possibly the only really safe affirmation is that the illiterates will not get by without a little help from their friends.

Does that mean you?

Suggested reading

The following publications are proposed as follow-up reading to the present booklet for three reasons: the interested but non-specialized reader can understand them with ease; they are short; and they may be had free of charge (by writing to the Office of Public Information, Unesco, Place de Fontenoy, 75700 Paris (France)). Each one exists in English, French and Spanish language versions.

Literacy and Development, by H. M. Phillips, Paris, Unesco, 1970.
A clear introduction to the following aspects of the literacy problem: motivations to literacy and its attainment; literacy and economic growth; and literacy and agricultural and industrial productivity.

World Congress of Ministers of Education on the Eradication of Illiteracy: Final Report, Unesco, 1965.
The general conclusion and general and commission recommendations of the landmark world gathering at which the functional approach to literacy gained widespread acceptance.

Functional Literacy: Why and How, Paris, Unesco, 1970.
A succinct introduction to the functional literacy concept, including its meaning, implementation, initial results, problems, and proposed future action relating to it.

Literacy: 1969–1971, Unesco, 1972.
A report on concrete progress achieved in literacy throughout the world in the last two years, focusing on: evolving views of literacy; new techniques and tools for making people literate; organization of literacy action; and literacy as a problem that transcends national boundaries. (Similar reports may be had for the years 1965–1967 and 1967–1969, respectively.)

Illiteracy and Human Rights, Paris, Unesco, 1968.
Three texts on illiteracy and human rights published on the

occasion of the International Year for Human Rights and entitled: 'One Must First be Able to Read'; 'Illiteracy: a Major Obstacle to the Effective Enjoyment of Human Rights'; and A resolution on illiteracy adopted by the Second Committee of the United Nations International Conference on Human Rights (1968).

Literacy: A Newsletter, Paris, Unesco, bi-monthly.

This periodical gives up-to-the-minute figures, news and features on literacy activities throughout the world, and will be sent on request to interested individuals and groups. Available in English, French and Spanish.

In addition to the above publications, Unesco has issued a number of technical manuals for organizers of literacy campaigns on subjects ranging from the construction, evaluation and use of literacy primers to the use, evaluation and production of filmstrips. These manuals are moderately priced. A list of those available may be had on request. Please be sure to specify the desired language.

Interested researchers may also write to the Documentalist, Unesco Literacy Division, for further information on literacy bibliography, particularly of a more technical nature.

Finally, the Secretariat of the Standing Committee of International Non-Governmental Organizations in Consultative Relations with Unesco (Office of NGO, Unesco, Place de Fontenoy, 75700 Paris (France)), may be contacted for information on publications it and its members have issued in relation to their work for literacy.